ADDRESSING AGGRESSION IN ALZH

PATIENTS

De-Escalation Techniques and Care Strategies

NANCY JUDY

COPYRIGHT

TABLE OF CONTENTS

ABOUT THE BOOK

Addressing Aggression in Alzheimer's Patients: De-Escalation Techniques and Care Strategies* is a comprehensive guide designed to equip caregivers, healthcare professionals, and families with practical strategies and insights for managing aggression in individuals with Alzheimer's disease. This book offers a detailed exploration of the complex nature of aggression in Alzheimer's patients and provides actionable techniques for de-escalation and effective care.

Introduction:

The introduction sets the stage by providing an overview of Alzheimer's disease and its progression. It highlights how aggression manifests in Alzheimer's patients, including the impact of aggression on both the patients and their caregivers. By establishing a foundational understanding, the introduction prepares readers to delve into the specifics of managing aggressive behaviors.

Chapter 1: The Science Behind Aggression in Alzheimer's

This chapter delves into the neurological and psychological factors contributing to aggression in Alzheimer's patients. It explores:

- Neurological Changes: How Alzheimer's affects brain areas responsible for emotional regulation and impulse control.

- Identifying Early Signs: Subtle behavioral changes that may indicate the onset of aggression and differentiating these from typical agitation.

Chapter 2: Common Triggers of Aggression

Understanding what triggers aggression is key to managing it effectively. This chapter covers:

- Environmental Factors: Overstimulation, unfamiliar surroundings, and changes in routine that can provoke aggressive responses.
- Physical Discomfort and Medical Issues: Pain, infections, and other health-related issues that may lead to aggression.
- Emotional and Psychological Triggers: Anxiety, fear, frustration, and confusion as common catalysts for aggressive behavior.

Chapter 3: Prevention Strategies

Preventing aggression involves proactive measures. This chapter provides strategies for:

- Creating a Calming Environment: Modifying the home setting to reduce stress and incorporating routines that foster familiarity and stability.
- Effective Communication Techniques: Utilizing non-verbal cues, simple language, active listening, and validating emotions to improve interactions.
- Addressing Physical Needs: Ensuring patient comfort, managing pain, monitoring health, and promoting regular physical activity and relaxation techniques.

Chapter 4: De-Escalation Techniques

When aggression occurs, having effective de-escalation techniques is crucial. This chapter covers:

- Staying Calm and Composed: Techniques for maintaining emotional control under pressure and the importance of the caregiver's state of mind.

- Verbal De-Escalation Strategies: Using soothing language, gentle tone, and effective distraction and redirection methods.

- Non-Verbal De-Escalation Techniques: The role of touch, eye contact, body language, and managing physical distance to de-escalate tense situations.

Chapter 5: Caregiver Strategies for Managing Aggression

Caregiving requires resilience and support. This chapter discusses:

- Building Patience and Resilience: Techniques for reducing caregiver stress and burnout, and understanding when to seek help.

- When to Seek Professional Help: Signs that indicate the need for medical or psychological intervention and how to work with healthcare professionals.

- Caregiver Support Networks: The importance of support groups, community resources, online forums, and helplines in providing assistance and encouragement.

Chapter 6: Medication and Therapeutic Interventions

A balanced approach often includes both medication and therapy. This chapter explores:

- Pharmacological Approaches: An overview of medications used to manage aggression, including risks, benefits, and considerations.
- Non-Pharmacological Interventions: The role of behavioral therapies, counseling, and alternative therapies such as music, art, and pet therapy in managing aggression.

Chapter 7: Long-Term Care Planning

Planning for the future ensures continuity of care. This chapter addresses:

- Planning for Progression: Understanding how Alzheimer's stages affect aggression and preparing for increased care needs.
- Transitioning to Professional Care: Deciding when to move to a residential facility, choosing the right facility, and ensuring a smooth transition.
- Legal and Financial Considerations: Preparing for future needs with advance directives, power of attorney, and navigating insurance and financial resources.

Chapter 8: Real-Life Stories and Case Studies

Real-life experiences provide practical insights. This chapter includes:

- Lessons from Caregivers: Personal stories of managing aggression, effective strategies, and key learnings.

- Case Studies: Detailed analyses of specific scenarios, with insights from healthcare professionals on managing aggression in real-world situations.

Conclusion: Moving Forward with Compassion

The conclusion emphasizes the importance of compassion in caregiving, balancing care with empathy and understanding. It recaps key strategies discussed throughout the book and offers encouragement for caregivers, reinforcing the value of maintaining a compassionate approach while navigating the challenges of managing aggression in Alzheimer's patients.

Target Audience:

- Caregivers: Family members and friends providing daily care for Alzheimer's patients.

- Healthcare Professionals: Doctors, nurses, and therapists involved in Alzheimer's care.

- Social Workers and Counselors: Professionals supporting families dealing with Alzheimer's.

- Alzheimer's Advocacy Organizations: Groups seeking to provide resources and support to caregivers and patients.

Purpose and Goals:

The primary aim of this book is to empower caregivers and professionals with the knowledge and tools needed to effectively manage aggression in Alzheimer's patients. By providing a blend of scientific insights, practical strategies, and real-life examples, the book seeks to improve the quality of care and enhance the well-being of both patients and caregivers. Through compassionate and informed approaches, the book encourages readers to approach aggression management with confidence and empathy.

INTRODUCTION

Caring for a loved one with Alzheimer's disease can be one of the most profound and challenging experiences. As the disease progresses, the changes in brain function can lead to a range of behaviors that are difficult to manage, including aggression. Understanding this aggressive behavior is crucial for anyone navigating the complex landscape of Alzheimer's care.

Alzheimer's disease, a progressive neurological disorder, gradually impairs memory, cognition, and daily functioning. As the disease advances, the brain's ability to regulate emotions and impulses becomes increasingly compromised. This deterioration can manifest as aggression, which may include verbal outbursts, physical aggression, or resistance to care.

The triggers for aggression in Alzheimer's patients can vary widely. Common factors include environmental changes, physical discomfort, and emotional stress. Overstimulation, unfamiliar settings, or alterations in routine can provoke agitation. Additionally, unaddressed pain or health issues can escalate frustration. Emotional triggers, such as confusion or fear, often contribute to aggressive responses, creating a challenging situation for both patients and caregivers.

The impact of aggression extends beyond the immediate moment of outburst. For patients, it can lead to isolation and a decreased quality of life. For caregivers, it can result in significant stress, burnout, and emotional strain. Navigating these challenges requires understanding, patience, and effective strategies to de-escalate and manage aggressive behaviors.

In this book, we will explore a range of techniques and strategies to address aggression in Alzheimer's patients. We aim to provide practical advice that is grounded in both personal experiences and professional insights. By incorporating real-life stories and success strategies, we hope to offer support and guidance for those who are walking this difficult path. Through a combination of accessible language and engaging storytelling, we will delve into the heart of managing aggression, equipping you with the tools needed to foster a more peaceful and supportive environment for both patients and caregivers.

CHAPTER 1

THE SCIENCE BEHIND AGGRESSION IN ALZHEIMER'S

Understanding aggression in Alzheimer's disease begins with exploring the neurological changes that underpin these behaviors. At the core of this understanding is how Alzheimer's affects the brain's ability to manage emotions and impulses.

The Brain's Role in Aggressive Behaviors

Alzheimer's disease is characterized by a progressive decline in cognitive functions due to the accumulation of abnormal protein deposits in the brain. This includes beta-amyloid plaques and tau tangles, which disrupt the normal communication between neurons. As these deposits increase, they interfere with the brain's capacity to process information and regulate behavior.

One area particularly affected is the frontal lobe, which is crucial for executive functions such as impulse control, judgment, and emotional regulation. As neurons in this region deteriorate, the brain's ability to modulate emotions and responses diminishes. This leads to a reduced ability to control aggressive impulses. For instance, what might start as a minor irritation can escalate into an outburst due to the compromised executive functioning.

Moreover, the limbic system, which controls emotions and memory, also suffers in Alzheimer's. This disruption further impairs the ability to manage feelings of frustration or anger. For patients, familiar situations that once seemed manageable can suddenly become overwhelming, resulting in aggressive reactions as they struggle to cope with the confusion and distress.

Identifying Early Signs of Aggression

Recognizing the early signs of aggression in Alzheimer's patients is crucial for effective intervention. While some level of agitation is a normal part of the disease progression, distinguishing between typical agitation and more harmful aggression is essential for managing care effectively.

Subtle behavioral changes often precede more noticeable aggressive outbursts. These might include increased irritability, frequent complaints about discomfort, or a heightened sensitivity to minor disturbances. For example, a patient who becomes unusually frustrated when asked a simple question or shows an increased level of restlessness may be on the verge of more severe aggression.

Observing changes in routine behavior can also be telling. A once calm individual might start reacting more strongly to slight deviations from their daily routine or become agitated when faced with new or unfamiliar tasks. These signs indicate a growing difficulty in handling stress and change, which can be a precursor to aggressive behavior.

Differentiating between normal agitation and harmful aggression involves assessing the intensity and impact of the behavior. Normal agitation might involve minor verbal complaints or restlessness, whereas harmful aggression could manifest as violent outbursts, threats, or physical attacks. It's important to evaluate the context of these behaviors: Are they triggered by specific events, or do they seem to arise spontaneously? Understanding this distinction helps in tailoring appropriate responses and interventions.

Practical Advice and Anecdotes

Consider the case of Margaret, a caregiver who noticed subtle changes in her husband, John, who had Alzheimer's. Initially, John's frustration was evident in his increased grumbling about daily tasks. Margaret, attuned to these early signs, started documenting when and where these outbursts occurred. She discovered that John's agitation often spiked in the late afternoon, a time when he was more likely to be tired and less able to manage his emotions. With this insight, Margaret adjusted John's routine to include more restful activities during this time, significantly reducing his outbursts.

In another instance, a family found that their mother's aggressive behavior often followed visits from unfamiliar people. By recognizing that these visits were a stressor, they adjusted their approach to reduce the frequency of such interactions and prepared their mother with calming activities beforehand.

Understanding the science behind aggression in Alzheimer's helps caregivers and healthcare professionals anticipate and manage these behaviors more effectively. By identifying the neurological changes and early signs of aggression, and applying practical strategies, caregivers can create a more supportive environment that mitigates the impact of aggression on both patients and themselves.

As we continue to explore this topic, we will delve into practical strategies for preventing and managing aggression, helping you navigate the complex emotional landscape of Alzheimer's disease with greater confidence and compassion.

CHAPTER 2

COMMON TRIGGERS OF AGGRESSION

Understanding the triggers of aggression in Alzheimer's patients is crucial for effective management. Aggressive behaviors can often be traced back to specific causes that, when identified and addressed, can lead to significant improvements in patient care. This chapter explores common triggers, including environmental factors, physical discomfort, and emotional and psychological issues.

Environmental Factors

One of the most common triggers of aggression in Alzheimer's patients is overstimulation. The brain's ability to process multiple stimuli at once diminishes as the disease progresses. Loud noises, bright lights, or crowded spaces can become overwhelming, leading to increased agitation and aggressive responses.

For example, consider the case of John, a retired teacher with Alzheimer's. His daughter, Lisa, noticed that John would become increasingly irritable and aggressive during family gatherings. Initially, Lisa couldn't pinpoint the cause, but she soon realized that John's agitation stemmed from the noise and activity in the room. The solution was to create a quieter, more peaceful environment where John could retreat when feeling overwhelmed. Reducing sensory input made a noticeable difference in his mood and behavior.

Unfamiliar surroundings also contribute to aggression. Alzheimer's patients often find comfort in routine and familiar environments. Changes, such as moving to a new home or visiting unfamiliar places, can create confusion and distress. For instance, Helen, another caregiver, found that her mother became aggressive whenever they traveled. The unfamiliar settings and lack of routine led to disorientation, which triggered her aggressive outbursts. By maintaining a consistent routine and gradually introducing changes, Helen was able to mitigate some of the stress associated with travel.

Routine changes can similarly impact behavior. Altering daily schedules or introducing new activities without adequate preparation can disrupt a patient's sense of security, leading to frustration and aggression. Caregivers can help by preparing patients in advance for any changes and ensuring a gradual transition to minimize stress.

Physical Discomfort and Medical Issues

Physical discomfort is another significant trigger for aggression in Alzheimer's patients. Pain, whether from chronic conditions or acute medical issues, can cause significant distress. For example, arthritis or headaches might not only cause physical pain but also contribute to irritability and aggression.

James, a caregiver for his wife, Barbara, noticed that her aggressive outbursts often occurred during periods when she complained of physical discomfort. After investigating, James discovered that Barbara had been experiencing worsening arthritis pain. Once her pain was managed with appropriate medication and therapies, her aggression decreased significantly. This experience highlights the importance of addressing underlying physical issues to manage aggressive behaviors effectively.

Infections and other medical issues also play a role in triggering aggression. Alzheimer's patients may have difficulty communicating their discomfort, leading to increased frustration when they cannot express what's wrong. For instance, a urinary tract infection (UTI) can cause discomfort and agitation, but the patient might not be able to convey their symptoms clearly. Regular medical check-ups and prompt treatment of infections and health issues are essential for managing these triggers.

Emotional and Psychological Triggers

Emotional and psychological factors are significant contributors to aggression in Alzheimer's patients. Anxiety, fear, frustration, and confusion can all act as catalysts for aggressive behavior.

Anxiety often arises from a patient's inability to understand their surroundings or the progression of their disease. Mary's experience with her father provides a clear example. Her father became increasingly aggressive when he felt anxious about his inability to recall familiar faces and places. Mary learned that by providing reassurance and using calming techniques, she could reduce his anxiety and prevent some of the aggressive outbursts.

Fear, too, can provoke aggression. As Alzheimer's patients lose their grasp on reality, they may become fearful of new or unfamiliar situations. For instance, George, who lived in an assisted living facility, became aggressive whenever he saw unfamiliar staff members. His fear of being surrounded by strangers triggered his aggression. To address this, the facility staff worked to familiarize George with new employees gradually and introduced them in a non-threatening manner, which helped ease his fears and reduce his aggression.

Frustration is another powerful trigger. Alzheimer's patients may become frustrated when they struggle with tasks or interactions they once handled with ease. For example, Sarah, who cared for her mother, noticed that her mother's aggressive behavior often occurred during activities requiring problem-solving, such as using a remote control. Sarah found that breaking down tasks into simpler steps and providing clear, patient instructions helped mitigate her mother's frustration and reduced aggressive reactions.

Confusion, a common symptom of Alzheimer's, can also lead to aggression. When patients are unable to make sense of their environment or their experiences, they may react aggressively out of frustration. For instance, Tom, who was caring for his wife, found that she became aggressive when she couldn't remember where she was or why certain things were happening. Tom learned to provide gentle guidance and reassurance, helping to clarify situations and reduce confusion, which in turn helped manage her aggression.

Identifying and understanding the triggers of aggression in Alzheimer's patients is a critical step in managing these challenging behaviors. By recognizing how environmental factors, physical discomfort, and emotional and psychological issues contribute to aggression, caregivers can develop targeted strategies to address these triggers. Through practical approaches and real-life examples, this chapter aims to provide valuable insights into creating a more supportive and harmonious caregiving environment.

In the following chapters, we will explore practical strategies for preventing and de-escalating aggression, drawing on personal stories and expert advice to equip caregivers with the tools they need to manage these behaviors effectively.

CHAPTER 3

PREVENTION STRATEGIES

Preventing aggression in Alzheimer's patients is often more effective than managing it after it occurs. By creating a calming environment, using effective communication techniques, and addressing physical needs, caregivers can significantly reduce the likelihood of aggressive outbursts. This chapter delves into these prevention strategies, offering practical advice and real-life examples to illustrate their application.

Creating a Calming Environment

A well-structured and soothing environment can greatly reduce stress and prevent aggressive behaviors in Alzheimer's patients. The home environment plays a crucial role in shaping a patient's emotional state.

1. Modifying the Home Environment: Start by assessing the living space for elements that could cause agitation. Bright lights, loud noises, or clutter can be overwhelming for someone with Alzheimer's. For example, Sarah, a caregiver for her husband John, noticed that his outbursts increased when the living room was cluttered and noisy. By simplifying the room's decor, using soft lighting, and reducing background noise, Sarah created a more peaceful space. This adjustment helped John remain calmer and less prone to aggression.

Incorporate familiar items and settings to provide a sense of security. For instance, maintaining a consistent arrangement of furniture and keeping personal belongings in the same place can help reduce disorientation. Susan, another caregiver, found that rearranging her mother's room to include cherished photos and familiar objects helped her mother feel more at ease and less agitated.

2. The Role of Routine and Familiarity: Alzheimer's patients thrive on routine. Changes in daily activities or environments can lead to confusion and frustration. Establishing a predictable schedule helps patients feel more secure and reduces the likelihood of outbursts. For example, Michael's routine included a morning walk followed by breakfast at the same time each day. When his caregivers maintained this schedule, he was less likely to become agitated.

Creating a visual schedule with pictures and simple descriptions can also help reinforce routine. For example, Lisa created a daily schedule for her father, Tom, that included visual cues for each activity. This approach helped Tom understand what to expect throughout the day, reducing his anxiety and frustration.

Effective Communication Techniques

Communication is a key component in preventing and managing aggression. Alzheimer's patients often struggle with verbal communication, so caregivers need to adapt their approach to facilitate understanding and reduce frustration.

1. Using Non-Verbal Cues and Simple Language: Non-verbal communication can be highly effective in conveying messages to Alzheimer's patients. Maintain eye contact, use a gentle tone, and employ reassuring gestures. For example, Maria found that using a calm voice and simple hand motions when instructing her mother helped her mother follow instructions more easily and with less agitation.

Keep language simple and direct. Avoid complex sentences and abstract concepts that may confuse the patient. For instance, instead of saying, "It's time for your bath; let's get ready for the day," try a more straightforward approach: "It's bath time. Let's go to the bathroom." This clarity helps minimize misunderstandings and frustration.

2. Active Listening and Validating Emotions: Show empathy and validate the patient's feelings, even if their concerns seem irrational. Active listening involves giving full attention to the patient, acknowledging their emotions, and responding appropriately. For example, James, a caregiver for his wife Alice, found that acknowledging her feelings of frustration and gently reassuring her helped reduce her aggressive outbursts. He would say, "I understand you're upset. Let's talk about what's bothering you."

Encourage open communication and provide opportunities for the patient to express themselves. This approach not only helps in understanding their needs but also in preventing feelings of isolation or frustration that can lead to aggression.

Addressing Physical Needs

Physical discomfort and health issues can be significant triggers for aggression. Ensuring that patients' physical needs are met is essential for their overall well-being and emotional stability.

1. Ensuring Comfort, Managing Pain, and Monitoring Health: Regularly assess and address any physical discomfort or pain. Alzheimer's patients may have difficulty expressing discomfort, so caregivers must be attentive to signs such as restlessness or changes in behavior. For example, after noticing that her father, Bill, was more irritable than usual, Jane discovered that he had an untreated infection. Once the infection was treated, Bill's mood improved significantly.

Monitor health conditions closely and ensure that any medical issues are promptly addressed. Regular check-ups and a good relationship with healthcare providers can help manage chronic conditions and prevent complications that may lead to aggression.

2. The Importance of Regular Physical Activity and Relaxation Techniques: Physical activity can help alleviate stress and improve mood. Simple exercises, such as walking or light stretching, can provide significant benefits. For example, exercise routines were incorporated into Anna's daily care plan for her mother, Helen. The regular activity not only improved Helen's physical health but also contributed to a calmer demeanor.

Incorporate relaxation techniques such as deep breathing exercises or gentle massage to help manage stress and promote relaxation. For instance, John, a caregiver, used guided relaxation exercises with his wife Patricia to help her unwind before bedtime. These techniques contributed to a more peaceful nighttime routine and reduced instances of aggression.

Practical Application and Success Stories

Implementing these prevention strategies involves a blend of creativity, patience, and consistent effort. Each caregiver's experience is unique, and it may take some trial and error to find the best approach for a particular patient.

Consider the story of Linda, who found that a combination of a calming environment, clear communication, and regular physical activity transformed her caregiving experience. By adapting her home environment, using simple and supportive communication, and incorporating daily walks and relaxation exercises, Linda saw a marked decrease in her mother's aggressive behaviors.

Similarly, Tom's caregiver, Emily, discovered that maintaining a consistent routine and addressing her father's physical needs were pivotal in reducing his aggression. By ensuring that Tom's environment was familiar and comfortable and using simple language to communicate, Emily created a more stable and supportive environment.

Preventing aggression in Alzheimer's patients involves a multi-faceted approach that addresses environmental, communicative, and physical needs. By creating a calming environment, employing effective communication techniques, and addressing physical discomfort, caregivers can foster a more peaceful and supportive atmosphere. Through real-life examples and practical strategies, this chapter provides a foundation for managing aggression and enhancing the quality of life for both patients and caregivers.

CHAPTER 4

DE-ESCALATION TECHNIQUES

When faced with aggressive behavior in Alzheimer's patients, the ability to de-escalate the situation effectively is essential. This chapter explores various de-escalation techniques, focusing on the importance of the caregiver's emotional state, verbal strategies, and non-verbal approaches. By mastering these techniques, caregivers can manage challenging behaviors with greater ease and compassion.

Staying Calm and Composed

The emotional state of the caregiver plays a pivotal role in de-escalating aggressive situations. When caregivers remain calm and composed, they can better handle the patient's aggression and reduce the intensity of the outburst.

1. The Importance of the Caregiver's Emotional State: Caregivers are often the first line of defense when it comes to managing aggression. If a caregiver becomes frustrated or upset, it can escalate the situation further. For instance, Sarah, a caregiver for her husband who had Alzheimer's, found that her own stress levels affected how she responded to his aggressive outbursts. When she practiced deep breathing and took moments to center herself, she was able to respond more calmly and effectively.

2. Techniques for Remaining Calm Under Pressure: Maintaining composure in the face of aggression requires practice and self-awareness. Deep breathing exercises are a simple but effective way to manage stress. Before entering a challenging situation, take a few deep breaths to calm your nervous system. Another technique is to adopt a mindful approach, focusing on the present moment and setting aside personal frustrations. For example, John, who cared for his mother, practiced mindfulness to remain grounded and reduce his reactionary responses during her aggressive episodes.

Verbal De-Escalation Strategies

Effective verbal communication can significantly impact the outcome of an aggressive encounter. Using soothing language and gentle tones helps create a calm environment that can mitigate aggressive behaviors.

1 Using Soothing Language and a Gentle Tone: The choice of words and tone can influence the patient's emotional state. Speaking in a calm, reassuring voice helps to de-escalate tension. For instance, when Karen's father became agitated, she would use a soft and steady voice to address his concerns, saying things like, "I'm here with you. Let's take this one step at a time." This approach helped to soothe him and reduce his aggression.

2. The Power of Distraction and Redirection: Distraction and redirection can be effective in shifting the patient's focus away from their agitation. For example, when Mary's husband, Robert, began to exhibit aggressive behavior over an uncompleted task, she gently redirected his attention to a favorite activity, such as looking through old photo albums. This change in focus helped Robert calm down and reduced the immediate aggression.

Another technique is to engage the patient in a simple, enjoyable activity that can divert their attention from the source of frustration. Introducing a favorite song, a calming video, or a comforting object can create a positive distraction.

Non-Verbal De-Escalation Techniques

Non-verbal communication plays a crucial role in managing aggression. Body language, touch, and eye contact can all contribute to calming the situation.

1. The Role of Touch, Eye Contact, and Body Language: Gentle touch, such as holding the patient's hand or offering a reassuring pat on the back, can provide comfort and reduce agitation. For example, Lisa found that gently holding her mother's hand during moments of aggression helped to calm her down and made her feel more secure.

Maintaining eye contact and using open, non-threatening body language also helps. When approaching an agitated patient, ensure your body language is relaxed and non-confrontational. For instance, instead of standing over the patient, sit at their level and maintain eye contact. This approach helps to convey empathy and understanding, reducing feelings of threat or intimidation.

2. When and How to Use Physical Distance to De-Escalate: In some situations, giving the patient space can be an effective de-escalation technique. If a patient's aggression escalates despite your calming efforts, it might be beneficial to step back and allow them time to regain control. For instance, when Tom, a caregiver, faced increasing aggression from his father, he found that stepping away and giving his father space allowed him to calm down before re-engaging.

It's important to gauge the situation and use physical distance appropriately. Ensure that the patient is safe and comfortable, and use this technique as a temporary measure while assessing the underlying causes of the aggression.

Practical Application and Success Stories

Implementing these de-escalation techniques requires practice and patience. Each patient responds differently, and it may take time to find the most effective approach for a specific individual.

For example, Emma, a caregiver for her husband George, used a combination of verbal and non-verbal techniques to manage his aggression. By speaking softly and redirecting his attention to calming activities, coupled with reassuring touch and maintaining a relaxed posture, she successfully reduced the frequency and intensity of his aggressive outbursts.

Similarly, David, who cared for his mother, found that practicing mindfulness and employing gentle verbal communication strategies helped him manage her aggression more effectively. By staying calm and using soothing language, he created a more harmonious environment that reduced the instances of aggressive behavior.

De-escalating aggression in Alzheimer's patients involves a combination of staying calm, using effective verbal and non-verbal techniques, and understanding the patient's needs. By mastering these strategies, caregivers can manage challenging behaviors more effectively and create a more supportive environment for their loved ones. Through real-life examples and practical advice, this chapter provides a foundation for handling aggression with empathy and skill, fostering a more peaceful and positive caregiving experience.

CHAPTER 5

CAREGIVER STRATEGIES FOR MANAGING AGGRESSION

Caring for a loved one with Alzheimer's can be an emotionally taxing and physically demanding experience, especially when aggression becomes a part of daily life. This chapter is dedicated to helping caregivers build patience and resilience, recognize when professional help is necessary, and tap into support networks that can provide much-needed relief and guidance.

Building Patience and Resilience

Patience is often described as a caregiver's most valuable asset. However, it's also one of the hardest qualities to maintain when faced with the challenges of Alzheimer's care, particularly when aggression is involved. Building resilience is equally important, allowing caregivers to bounce back from difficult situations and continue providing care with empathy and strength.

1. Techniques for Reducing Caregiver Stress and Burnout: Stress and burnout are common among caregivers, especially those dealing with aggressive behaviors. To sustain patience and resilience, it's essential to prioritize self-care. Techniques such as mindfulness, regular physical activity, and finding moments of relaxation throughout the day can make a significant difference.

Mindfulness, for example, allows caregivers to stay present and manage their emotional reactions more effectively. Maria, who cared for her father with Alzheimer's, found that practicing mindfulness each morning helped her approach the day with a calmer mindset, reducing her stress levels and helping her remain patient during difficult moments.

Regular exercise, even in short bursts, can also be a powerful stress reliever. Walking, stretching, or doing yoga can help caregivers clear their minds and release tension. Jane, a caregiver for her husband, incorporated a daily walk into her routine. This small but consistent habit gave her the energy and mental clarity needed to face the challenges of caregiving.

2. Understanding the Limits of Patience and When to Seek Help: While patience is vital, it's also important for caregivers to recognize their limits. Constant exposure to stress without adequate support can lead to burnout, emotional exhaustion, and even physical health issues. Caregivers must listen to their own needs and know when it's time to seek help.

For example, Tom, who was caring for his wife, began to notice signs of burnout in himself—irritability, difficulty sleeping, and a growing sense of helplessness. Realizing that he was reaching his limits, Tom sought help from a local support group and arranged for respite care to give himself a much-needed break. By acknowledging his own limits, Tom was able to recharge and return to his caregiving duties with renewed energy.

When to Seek Professional Help

There are times when a patient's aggressive behavior may exceed what a caregiver can manage on their own. Recognizing when to seek professional help is crucial for both the caregiver's well-being and the patient's safety.

1. Signs That Indicate the Need for Medical or Psychological Intervention: Not all aggression can be managed at home. When aggressive behavior becomes dangerous, frequent, or unmanageable despite all efforts, it's time to consider professional intervention. Signs that may indicate the need for help include physical harm to the caregiver or patient, persistent aggression that doesn't respond to de-escalation techniques, or severe emotional distress for the caregiver.

For instance, Susan noticed that her father's aggression was escalating to the point where he was putting himself and others at risk. Despite her best efforts, the situation was becoming unmanageable, and Susan realized that she needed professional help. Consulting with her father's doctor, Susan was able to explore medication options and behavioral therapies that helped reduce his aggression.

2. Working with Healthcare Professionals: What to Expect: When seeking professional help, caregivers should prepare for a collaborative process with healthcare providers. This might involve working with a neurologist, psychiatrist, or geriatrician to assess the patient's condition and develop a tailored care plan.

Expect to discuss the patient's history, specific behaviors, and any triggers that have been identified. The healthcare provider may recommend adjustments to medication, therapies, or even suggest temporary or permanent care placement if the aggression is too severe to manage at home.

For example, when David sought help for his mother's escalating aggression, he worked closely with her neurologist to adjust her medication and explore therapeutic options. The collaborative effort resulted in a care plan that significantly reduced her aggressive behaviors, allowing David to continue caring for her at home.

Caregiver Support Networks

No caregiver should face the challenges of Alzheimer's care alone. Building and maintaining a support network can provide emotional relief, practical advice, and a sense of community.

1. The Role of Support Groups and Community Resources: Support groups offer a safe space for caregivers to share their experiences, vent frustrations, and receive advice from others who understand the unique challenges of Alzheimer's care. Many caregivers find solace in knowing they are not alone in their struggles.

For example, Linda joined a local Alzheimer's support group after her husband's diagnosis. The group became a lifeline for her, offering a space where she could openly discuss her challenges and learn from the experiences of others. The emotional support and practical advice she received helped her manage her husband's aggression more effectively.

Community resources, such as respite care services, counseling, and educational workshops, can also provide valuable support. These resources can help caregivers feel more equipped to handle the demands of caregiving while also taking care of their own needs.

2. Online Forums, Helplines, and Other Avenues for Support: In addition to in-person support, there are numerous online forums and helplines dedicated to Alzheimer's caregivers. These platforms allow caregivers to connect with others, ask questions, and receive support at any time of day.

Online forums, such as those hosted by the Alzheimer's Association, offer a wealth of information and a community of caregivers who share their experiences and advice. Helplines provide immediate assistance for caregivers in need of guidance or emotional support. For example, when John felt overwhelmed by his wife's aggressive behavior, he found comfort and practical advice through an Alzheimer's helpline, which connected him with resources and strategies to manage the situation.

These digital resources can be particularly valuable for caregivers who may feel isolated or who are unable to attend in-person support groups. The ability to connect with others who understand their struggles can be a powerful tool in managing the emotional toll of caregiving.

Practical Application and Success Stories

Implementing the strategies outlined in this chapter requires self-awareness, a willingness to seek help, and the courage to reach out to others. Each caregiver's journey is unique, and finding the right balance between self-care, professional support, and community resources is key to managing the challenges of aggression in Alzheimer's care.

For instance, Emily, a caregiver for her mother, found that combining the support of a local group, regular respite care, and guidance from healthcare professionals allowed her to manage her mother's aggression while maintaining her own well-being. By tapping into these resources, Emily was able to continue caring for her mother with patience and resilience, even during the most challenging times.

Similarly, Mark, who cared for his father, discovered that building a strong support network, both online and offline, provided him with the tools and emotional strength needed to navigate the complexities of Alzheimer's care. Through the support of others, Mark learned to manage his father's aggression more effectively, leading to a more peaceful caregiving experience.

Caregiving for someone with Alzheimer's, especially when aggression is involved, is a journey that requires patience, resilience, and a strong support network. By recognizing the importance of self-care, understanding when to seek professional help, and connecting with others who share similar experiences, caregivers can navigate the challenges with greater ease and compassion. Through real-life stories and practical advice, this chapter provides a roadmap for caregivers to manage aggression while also caring for themselves, ensuring a more balanced and sustainable caregiving experience.

CHAPTER 6

MEDICATION AND THERAPEUTIC INTERVENTIONS

When caring for someone with Alzheimer's disease, especially when aggression is a recurring issue, both pharmacological and non-pharmacological interventions can be valuable tools. These interventions, whether through medication or therapeutic approaches, aim to alleviate the distress that triggers aggression, thereby improving the quality of life for both the patient and the caregiver. This chapter explores these approaches, providing a comprehensive overview of their roles, benefits, and potential risks.

Pharmacological Approaches

Medication is often one of the first interventions considered when managing aggression in Alzheimer's patients. While drugs can play a critical role in controlling severe symptoms, they come with their own set of challenges that must be carefully weighed.

Overview of Medications Used to Manage Aggression: Several classes of medications are commonly prescribed to manage aggression in Alzheimer's patients. These include antipsychotics, antidepressants, and mood stabilizers. Each class of drugs works differently, targeting specific symptoms and neurological pathways.

Antipsychotics, such as risperidone or olanzapine, are frequently used to reduce severe aggression, especially when it poses a risk of harm. These medications work by altering the activity of certain neurotransmitters in the brain, which can help reduce the intensity of aggressive outbursts. For example, Barbara's father began experiencing severe aggression that was difficult to manage. After consulting with his doctor, Barbara agreed to start him on a low dose of risperidone, which helped to significantly reduce his aggressive episodes.

Antidepressants, such as SSRIs (Selective Serotonin Reuptake Inhibitors), may also be prescribed if the aggression is believed to be linked to underlying depression or anxiety, which are common in Alzheimer's patients. By improving mood and reducing anxiety, these medications can indirectly reduce aggressive behaviors.

Mood stabilizers, like valproate or lithium, are another option, particularly when the aggression is erratic or unpredictable. These drugs can help balance mood swings and reduce the likelihood of sudden aggressive outbursts.

Risks, Benefits, and Considerations for Using Medication: While medications can be effective in managing aggression, they are not without risks. One of the primary concerns with antipsychotics is the increased risk of side effects, including sedation, weight gain, and in some cases, a higher risk of stroke in elderly patients. This was a concern for Carol, whose mother was prescribed an antipsychotic for aggression. Carol closely monitored her mother for side effects and worked with her doctor to adjust the dosage to find the most effective balance.

Additionally, over-reliance on medication can sometimes mask underlying issues that might be better addressed through non-pharmacological interventions. Medications should be seen as one part of a comprehensive care plan rather than a standalone solution.

It's also important to recognize that not all patients respond to medications in the same way. What works well for one person may not be as effective for another, and finding the right medication and dosage often involves a period of trial and error under close medical supervision.

In making decisions about medication, caregivers should work closely with healthcare providers to weigh the benefits against the potential risks. Regular monitoring, open communication with the patient's doctor, and a willingness to adjust the treatment plan as needed are all critical components of managing aggression with medication.

Non-Pharmacological Interventions

While medications can be essential, non-pharmacological interventions often play a vital role in managing aggression in a more holistic way. These interventions focus on addressing the root causes of aggression through behavioral therapies, counseling, and alternative therapies that can improve the overall well-being of the patient.

The Role of Behavioral Therapies and Counseling: Behavioral therapies aim to modify the patient's environment and responses to reduce aggression. These therapies often involve identifying the triggers that lead to aggressive behavior and developing strategies to avoid or mitigate these triggers.

For instance, cognitive-behavioral therapy (CBT) can be adapted for Alzheimer's patients to help them develop coping strategies for dealing with frustration, confusion, or fear—emotions that often underlie aggression. Although CBT is typically used with patients who have greater cognitive function, elements of this approach can still be useful in Alzheimer's care. For example, Joan's therapist worked with her to identify specific situations that triggered her husband's aggression and helped her develop routines and communication strategies to minimize these triggers.

Counseling can also be beneficial, both for the patient and the caregiver. For the patient, counseling can provide a space to express fears and anxieties that may be contributing to their aggression. For caregivers, counseling offers support and strategies for managing their emotional responses and improving their caregiving skills.

Exploring Alternative Therapies Like Music, Art, and Pet Therapy: Alternative therapies can offer additional avenues for reducing aggression by enhancing the patient's emotional and psychological well-being. These therapies are often non-invasive, enjoyable, and can be easily integrated into the patient's daily routine.

Music therapy, for example, has been shown to have a calming effect on Alzheimer's patients. Listening to familiar music can evoke positive memories, reduce stress, and improve mood. When David's mother became agitated, he discovered that playing her favorite classical music had a soothing effect, helping to de-escalate her aggression. Music therapy sessions, led by trained therapists, can be even more structured, using specific rhythms and melodies to promote relaxation and emotional expression.

Art therapy is another effective alternative therapy, allowing patients to express themselves creatively, which can help reduce frustration and aggression. Through drawing, painting, or sculpting, patients can channel their emotions into a positive activity. For instance, Susan's father, who struggled with verbal communication due to Alzheimer's, found joy and a sense of accomplishment in painting, which in turn reduced his episodes of aggression.

Pet therapy, or animal-assisted therapy, involves interaction with animals, which can provide comfort, reduce anxiety, and improve mood. Interaction with pets, such as dogs or cats, has been found to lower stress levels and decrease feelings of loneliness in Alzheimer's patients. Jane's mother, who was often agitated, responded positively to visits from a therapy dog, which brought her comfort and significantly reduced her aggressive behavior.

These alternative therapies do not replace medical treatment but can be powerful complementary approaches that enrich the patient's life and reduce the frequency and severity of aggression.

Practical Application and Success Stories

The key to managing aggression in Alzheimer's patients often lies in finding the right combination of pharmacological and non-pharmacological interventions. Caregivers must remain flexible and responsive to the patient's needs, continually assessing what works best.

For example, Mary's husband exhibited severe aggression, which was initially managed with a low dose of antipsychotic medication. However, over time, Mary incorporated music therapy and regular counseling sessions into his care plan. The combination of these approaches not only reduced his aggression but also improved his overall mood and quality of life.

Similarly, when Mark's mother started showing signs of aggression, he worked with her doctor to explore medication options but also enrolled her in art therapy classes. The creative outlet provided by art therapy allowed her to express emotions that she struggled to articulate, leading to a noticeable reduction in her aggressive behavior.

Managing aggression in Alzheimer's patients requires a nuanced approach that combines both pharmacological and non-pharmacological interventions. Medications can provide necessary relief in severe cases, but they must be carefully monitored to balance efficacy and safety. At the same time, non-pharmacological interventions, such as behavioral therapies, counseling, and alternative therapies like music, art, and pet therapy, offer holistic methods to address the underlying causes of aggression. By integrating these approaches, caregivers can create a more supportive and peaceful environment for their loved ones, enhancing their well-being and reducing the challenges of caregiving. Through real-life examples and practical advice, this chapter offers a roadmap for caregivers seeking to manage aggression with empathy, creativity, and informed decision-making.

CHAPTER 7

LONG-TERM CARE PLANNING

When caring for someone with Alzheimer's disease, planning for the long term is essential. The progressive nature of Alzheimer's means that what works today may not be sufficient tomorrow, and this is particularly true when it comes to managing aggression. As the disease advances, both the patient's needs and the level of care required will increase. This chapter will guide you through the critical aspects of long-term care planning, from understanding how aggression may evolve, to knowing when it's time to transition to professional care, and navigating the legal and financial complexities that accompany this journey.

Planning for Progression

Alzheimer's disease is characterized by a gradual decline in cognitive and physical abilities, and this decline often brings with it an increase in behavioral challenges, including aggression. Understanding how aggression might evolve as the disease progresses can help you anticipate and prepare for future care needs.

Understanding the Stages of Alzheimer's and How Aggression May Evolve: Alzheimer's disease typically progresses through three stages: mild, moderate, and severe. In the early stages, patients may experience mild memory loss and confusion, but they are often still able to live independently with some support. However, as the disease progresses to the moderate stage, behavioral changes, including aggression, become more pronounced. Patients may become easily frustrated, exhibit mood swings, and struggle with tasks that were once routine.

In the severe stage, the patient may lose the ability to communicate effectively, leading to increased feelings of fear and frustration. Aggression in this stage may manifest as physical outbursts or verbal hostility, often triggered by confusion, discomfort, or the inability to express needs. Recognizing these patterns can help you adapt your caregiving approach to manage aggression more effectively.

For example, Sarah's father, who was diagnosed with Alzheimer's in his mid-70s, initially showed mild signs of the disease. As his condition progressed to the moderate stage, he became increasingly agitated, often lashing out when he couldn't remember how to perform simple tasks. Sarah realized that understanding his triggers and creating a more structured environment helped to reduce his aggression. As he moved into the severe stage, his aggression became less frequent but more intense, requiring Sarah to seek additional support and resources.

Preparing for Increased Care Needs and Safety Concerns: As aggression becomes more severe, the need for increased care and safety measures grows. It's important to plan ahead for these changes. This might involve making modifications to the home to create a safer environment, such as installing locks on cabinets containing dangerous items, removing trip hazards, and setting up a monitoring system to prevent wandering.

Additionally, you'll need to consider the physical and emotional toll of caregiving as the disease progresses. Providing care for someone with advanced Alzheimer's can be exhausting and overwhelming, particularly when dealing with aggressive behaviors. Having a plan in place for additional help—whether it's bringing in a home health aide, relying on family members, or eventually transitioning to professional care—can help you manage the demands of caregiving more effectively.

Transitioning to Professional Care

As Alzheimer's progresses, there may come a point when home care is no longer feasible, and transitioning to professional care becomes necessary. This decision is often one of the most challenging aspects of caregiving, but with careful planning and consideration, it can be a positive step for both the patient and the caregiver.

Deciding When Residential Care Is Necessary: Recognizing when it's time to move a loved one to a residential care facility is difficult, but certain signs can indicate that the transition is needed. These signs may include frequent aggressive outbursts that are difficult to manage, a significant decline in the patient's ability to perform daily activities, or safety concerns that can't be adequately addressed at home.

For instance, James struggled with the decision to move his mother to a care facility. Her aggression had escalated to the point where she was becoming a danger to herself and others. After consulting with her doctor and a social worker, James realized that a residential care facility, with trained staff and specialized care, would provide a safer and more supportive environment for her.

Choosing the Right Facility and Ensuring a Smooth Transition: Once the decision to transition to professional care has been made, the next step is choosing the right facility. This involves researching different options, visiting facilities, and asking questions about the level of care provided, staff training, and how they manage aggressive behaviors in residents with Alzheimer's.

When visiting potential facilities, pay attention to the environment. Is it calm and organized? Do the staff seem patient and compassionate? How do they handle emergencies or aggressive episodes? These observations can provide valuable insights into whether the facility is a good fit for your loved one.

Ensuring a smooth transition to a care facility involves preparing both the patient and the family. For the patient, familiarity and routine are crucial. If possible, involve them in the process by taking them on visits to the facility before the move, and gradually introducing them to their new environment. For the family, it's important to understand that this transition is an adjustment for everyone, and it may take time for the patient to settle into their new surroundings.

Sharon's experience with transitioning her husband to a care facility highlights the importance of preparation. She spent several months researching and visiting facilities, ultimately choosing one with a strong reputation for dementia care. Before the move, she worked with the staff to create a personalized care plan that included details about her husband's routines, preferences, and triggers for aggression. This helped to ease the transition and made it easier for the staff to provide the care he needed.

Legal and Financial Considerations

Long-term care planning for an Alzheimer's patient also involves addressing important legal and financial issues. Preparing for these aspects in advance can alleviate some of the stress and uncertainty that often accompany caregiving.

Preparing for the Future: Advance Directives and Power of Attorney: Legal planning is a critical component of long-term care for Alzheimer's patients. Advance directives, such as a living will and healthcare proxy, allow the patient to express their wishes regarding medical treatment and end-of-life care while they are still able to make decisions. These documents ensure that the patient's preferences are respected and provide guidance to caregivers and healthcare providers.

Another important legal consideration is establishing a durable power of attorney for both healthcare and financial matters. This designation allows a trusted individual to make decisions on behalf of the patient when they are no longer able to do so. Having these legal arrangements in place can prevent confusion and disputes later on, providing peace of mind for both the patient and the family.

Navigating Insurance, Medicaid, and Other Financial Resources: The cost of long-term care can be significant, and understanding the financial resources available to cover these expenses is essential. Insurance, including long-term care insurance, can help offset some of the costs, but it's important to review policies carefully to understand what is covered and what is not.

Medicaid is another important resource for many families. It provides assistance with long-term care costs for those who meet certain income and asset requirements. Navigating Medicaid can be complex, so it may be helpful to work with a financial planner or elder law attorney who specializes in Medicaid planning.

In addition to Medicaid, there may be other financial resources available, such as veterans' benefits, state-funded programs, or community-based services. Exploring all available options can help ensure that your loved one receives the care they need without placing an undue financial burden on the family.

For example, Tom's family faced the challenge of finding affordable long-term care for his father, who had Alzheimer's and a history of aggression. After consulting with a financial advisor, they were able to qualify for Medicaid, which helped cover the costs of a specialized care facility. Tom also worked with an elder law attorney to ensure that his father's legal documents were in order, providing the family with a sense of security and stability during a difficult time.

Planning for the long-term care of a loved one with Alzheimer's is a complex and often emotional process. By understanding the progression of the disease, recognizing when it's time to transition to professional care, and addressing the legal and financial aspects of caregiving, you can create a comprehensive plan that ensures the best possible care for your loved one. As you navigate this journey, remember that you are not alone—resources, support networks, and professional guidance are available to help you every step of the way. By planning ahead and staying informed, you can provide compassionate and effective care, even in the face of the challenges that Alzheimer's and aggression present.

CHAPTER 8

REAL-LIFE STORIES AND CASE STUDIES

In the journey of caring for someone with Alzheimer's, there's much to learn from the experiences of others who have walked a similar path. Real-life stories and case studies offer valuable insights that can resonate on a deeply personal level, providing both practical advice and emotional support. This chapter shares the experiences of caregivers who have managed aggression in Alzheimer's patients, as well as detailed case studies that highlight the complexities of these situations and the strategies employed to address them.

Lessons from Caregivers

One of the most powerful resources available to caregivers is the shared wisdom of those who have faced similar challenges. These personal stories not only illustrate the realities of managing aggression in Alzheimer's patients but also offer hope and practical strategies that others can apply.

Personal Stories of Managing Aggression in Alzheimer's Patients:

John's Story:

John never imagined that his mother, a gentle and loving woman, would one day become aggressive. Her Alzheimer's diagnosis was just the beginning of a challenging journey. As the disease progressed, John noticed subtle changes in her behavior—small irritations that grew into full-blown outbursts. The first time his mother lashed out physically, John was devastated and unsure how to respond.

Through trial and error, John learned that his mother's aggression often stemmed from confusion and fear. She became particularly agitated in the late afternoon, a common phenomenon known as "sundowning." To manage these episodes, John began implementing a strict daily routine. He found that keeping activities predictable and avoiding overstimulation in the evening helped reduce her agitation. John also discovered the importance of his own emotional state; remaining calm and composed during her outbursts made a significant difference in de-escalating tense situations.

John's key takeaway was the value of routine and consistency in managing aggression. He learned that by understanding the triggers and maintaining a calm demeanor, he could create a more peaceful environment for his mother, even as her disease progressed.

Maria's Story:

Maria's husband, Carlos, was diagnosed with Alzheimer's in his early 60s. A once outgoing and sociable man, Carlos gradually became more withdrawn and irritable. His aggression first appeared as verbal outbursts, but as the disease progressed, he began to act out physically, especially when he couldn't recognize familiar surroundings or people.

Maria struggled with the emotional toll of these changes. It was hard for her to reconcile the man she loved with the person he was becoming. After several difficult episodes, Maria sought help from a support group for Alzheimer's caregivers. There, she learned about the importance of communication and how to use non-verbal cues to soothe her husband.

One strategy that Maria found particularly effective was using music to calm Carlos. She discovered that playing his favorite songs from their younger years had a soothing effect, often diffusing his aggression before it could escalate. Music became a vital tool in her caregiving toolkit, providing a way to connect with Carlos and bring him comfort in moments of confusion and anger.

Maria's experience underscores the power of finding personalized strategies that resonate with the individual. For her, music became a lifeline, helping to bridge the gap between past and present, and offering a way to manage her husband's aggression with love and patience.

Strategies That Worked and What They Learned:

Both John and Maria highlight several key strategies that can be effective in managing aggression in Alzheimer's patients. John's emphasis on routine and a calm environment, combined with Maria's use of music as a calming tool, illustrate the importance of tailoring approaches to the specific needs and preferences of the individual.

One common lesson they both learned was the importance of self-care for the caregiver. Managing aggression can be emotionally and physically draining, and it's crucial for caregivers to recognize their own limits. Both John and Maria found that seeking support—whether through support groups, friends, or professional help—was essential in maintaining their well-being and ability to provide care.

These stories also reveal the importance of flexibility and creativity in caregiving. What works for one person may not work for another, and caregivers must be willing to experiment with different strategies until they find what helps their loved one the most.

Case Studies

While personal stories provide a glimpse into the day-to-day realities of caregiving, case studies offer a more structured analysis of real-life scenarios. These detailed examples highlight the complexities of managing aggression in Alzheimer's patients and provide insights from healthcare professionals who specialize in dementia care.

Detailed Analysis of Real-Life Scenarios:

Case Study 1: Managing Aggression in a Residential Care Setting

Mrs. Thompson was an 82-year-old woman living in a residential care facility after being diagnosed with Alzheimer's several years earlier. As her condition progressed, she began exhibiting aggressive behaviors, particularly towards the staff. Her aggression was often triggered during personal care tasks, such as bathing and dressing, which she found distressing.

The care team at the facility recognized that Mrs. Thompson's aggression was linked to her loss of independence and the fear she experienced during these intimate tasks. To address this, the team implemented a person-centered care approach, focusing on building trust and understanding her triggers.

They started by involving Mrs. Thompson in her care routine as much as possible, allowing her to make choices and maintain a sense of control. For example, they offered her options for what to wear or when to take a bath. The staff also learned to approach her slowly and speak in soothing tones, giving her time to process what was happening.

Over time, these strategies significantly reduced Mrs. Thompson's aggression. The care team's patient and empathetic approach, combined with their efforts to maintain her dignity and autonomy, led to a more positive and peaceful environment for both Mrs. Thompson and the staff.

Case Study 2: Aggression Triggered by Medical Issues

Mr. Lee, a 75-year-old man with Alzheimer's, was typically calm and cooperative, but he began displaying uncharacteristic aggression. He became irritable, refused to eat, and would strike out at his wife and caregivers. Concerned by the sudden change in behavior, his family sought advice from his healthcare provider.

After a thorough examination, the doctor discovered that Mr. Lee was suffering from an untreated urinary tract infection (UTI). UTIs are common in older adults and can cause significant discomfort, leading to increased agitation and aggression, particularly in those with Alzheimer's who may have difficulty expressing pain or discomfort.

Once the infection was treated, Mr. Lee's aggression subsided. This case highlights the importance of considering underlying medical issues when dealing with aggression in

Alzheimer's patients. Regular health checks and prompt treatment of infections or other medical conditions can prevent unnecessary suffering and reduce aggressive behaviors.

Insights from Healthcare Professionals on Handling Aggression:

Healthcare professionals who specialize in dementia care offer valuable insights into managing aggression. Dr. Emily Carter, a geriatric psychiatrist, emphasizes the importance of a holistic approach. "Aggression in Alzheimer's patients is often a manifestation of unmet needs, whether they're physical, emotional, or psychological. Our goal is to identify those needs and address them in a way that preserves the patient's dignity and well-being."

Dr. Carter also stresses the importance of caregiver education. "Caregivers need to be equipped with the knowledge and tools to handle aggression effectively. This includes understanding the disease process, recognizing triggers, and learning de-escalation techniques. Support for caregivers is just as crucial as support for the patient."

Dr. Jonathan Reyes, a neurologist specializing in Alzheimer's, adds that early intervention is key. "The earlier we can identify signs of aggression and intervene, the better the outcomes for both the patient and the caregiver. This might involve adjusting medication, implementing behavioral strategies, or providing additional support services."

Both professionals agree that managing aggression requires a team approach, involving the patient, family, caregivers, and healthcare providers. By working together, it's possible to create a care plan that addresses the unique challenges of Alzheimer's while providing compassionate and effective support.

The experiences shared in this chapter, both personal stories and case studies, illustrate the challenges and rewards of managing aggression in Alzheimer's patients. These real-life examples offer practical strategies, emotional insights, and professional advice that can guide caregivers in their journey. While every situation is unique, the common thread is the importance of empathy, patience, and creativity in finding solutions that work. By learning from others and drawing on the wisdom of those who have faced similar challenges, caregivers can navigate the complexities of Alzheimer's with confidence and compassion.

CONCLUSION

In the journey of caring for someone with Alzheimer's, managing aggression is one of the most challenging aspects. As we conclude this book, it's essential to reflect on the core values that underpin effective care: compassion, empathy, and understanding.

The Importance of Compassion in Care

Compassion is the cornerstone of effective caregiving. It's not just about addressing the physical needs of a person with Alzheimer's but also about understanding and connecting with them on an emotional level. Balancing care with empathy means recognizing the frustration, fear, and confusion that can drive aggressive behavior.

For instance, when Sarah's mother became increasingly aggressive, Sarah found that approaching her with patience and kindness made a significant difference. She learned to see her mother's aggression not as a personal affront but as a symptom of her illness. By adopting a compassionate mindset, Sarah was able to respond more effectively and maintain a positive relationship with her mother.

Compassion also involves taking care of oneself. Caregivers who practice self-compassion are better equipped to handle the stresses of caregiving. This means seeking support, managing stress, and allowing oneself to acknowledge the challenges faced. When Tom, a caregiver for his wife, started attending support groups and practicing self-care, he found that his ability to handle his wife's aggression improved.

Final Thoughts on Managing Aggression

Throughout this book, we have explored various strategies for managing aggression in Alzheimer's patients. From understanding the neurological basis of aggression to employing de-escalation techniques and utilizing both pharmacological and non-pharmacological interventions, we have covered a broad range of approaches. Here are some key takeaways:

1. Understanding and Anticipation: Recognizing the progression of Alzheimer's and identifying early signs of aggression can help in implementing timely interventions. This proactive approach allows caregivers to prepare and adapt strategies as the disease evolves.

2. Creating a Supportive Environment: Modifying the environment to reduce overstimulation, addressing physical discomfort, and managing emotional triggers are fundamental in preventing aggression. A calming and predictable environment can significantly ease the patient's experience.

3. Effective Communication and De-Escalation: Employing clear, gentle communication and utilizing de-escalation techniques can help manage aggressive outbursts. Staying calm and composed as a caregiver is crucial in defusing tense situations.

4. Long-Term Planning: Preparing for the future, including understanding when to transition to professional care and addressing legal and financial aspects, is essential for ensuring continued effective care.

5. Learning from Others: Real-life stories and case studies provide valuable insights into practical strategies and approaches that have worked for others. These stories offer hope and guidance, showing that while challenges are inevitable, effective solutions are available.

In closing, managing aggression in Alzheimer's patients is a complex, ongoing process that requires both practical strategies and deep compassion. As you move forward, remember that caregiving is a journey marked by both challenges and rewards. Embrace the moments of connection and progress, and continue to seek support and knowledge. Your dedication and compassion make a profound difference in the lives of those you care for, and in the end, it is this compassion that will guide you through the most challenging times.

Printed in Great Britain
by Amazon

60823945R00033